The **Hare** and the **Tortoise**

AND

The Fox
and the
Goat

Text adapted by
Amelia Marshall

Illustrated by
Liliane Oser &
Andy Rowland

W
FRANKLIN WATTS
LONDON•SYDNEY

The Hare
and the
Tortoise

Illustrated by Andy Rowland

Hare and Tortoise were
in the woods.

You are
so slow,
Tortoise!

I bet I can beat you in a race, Hare!

No way! I am much faster than you!

So Hare and Tortoise got ready for the big race.

The race began!

Tortoise crawled along slowly ...

... while Hare took a nap!

Tortoise kept going until she crossed the line!

7

Then Tortoise took a nap.

Meanwhile Hare woke up and started to run!

But he was too late!

Tortoise had already won.

Hooray for Tortoise!

Puzzle

Which words best describe
each character?

1. (Steady)

2. (Foolish)

3. (Proud)

4. (Boastful)

5. (Cunning)

6. (Eager)

Story Quiz

1. What does Tortoise bet he can do?

2. Why does Hare think he will win?

3. What does Hare do at the start of the race?

4. Who reaches the finish line first?

5. What did Hare learn?

The Fox
and the
Goat

Illustrated by Liliane Oser

Once upon a time, a fox fell into a well. He was stuck!

A goat walked up to the well.

I need some water!

Fox saw the goat and smiled.
He knew how to get out.

It looks nice
down there.

It's lovely.
Why don't you
join me?

Goat looked down.
The water looked
cool and fresh.

SPLASH! Goat dived in.

Now Goat was stuck in the well, too.

How are you going to get out, Goat?

Let me climb on your back, so I can get some help.

So Fox climbed up Goat and out of the well.

It's my turn, Fox. Get me out!

17

But Fox ran far away, leaving Goat stuck. Fox had tricked silly Goat!

Il'l help you, Goat!

Puzzle

Who says it? Match the chacracters
with their speech bubbles.

1. Get me out!

2. Why don't you join me?

3. I need some water.

4. I can get help.

5. It looks nice down there.

6. How are you going to get out?

Story Quiz

1. Why does Goat go to the well?

2. How does Fox encourage Goat?

3. What does Goat do?

4. How does Fox escape from the well?

5. Who is the cleverest character?

Answers

The Hare and the Tortoise

Puzzle (page 10)
Hare: 2, 3, 4
Tortoise: 1, 5, 6

Story Quiz (page 11)
1. Win a race against Hare
2. Because Tortoise is very slow
3. Takes a nap
4. Tortoise
5. Not to take things for granted

The Fox and the Goat

Puzzle (page 20)
Fox: 2, 4, 6
Goat: 1, 3, 5

Story Quiz (page 21)
1. Goat is hot and thirsty
2. Fox tells Goat the water is lovely
3. Goat jumps into the well
4. Fox climbs up Goat's back
5. Fox

Franklin Watts

First published in Great Britain in 2016 by
The Watts Publishing Group

Text © Franklin Watts 2016
Illustrations for The Fox and the Goat © Liliane Oser 2009
Illustrations for The Hare and the Tortoise © Andy Rowland 2009

The rights of Amelia Marshall to be identified as the author
and Liliane Oser and Andy Rowland as the illustrators of this Work
have been asserted in accordance with the Copyright,
Designs and Patents Act, 1988.

Series Editor: Melaie Palmer
Series Designer: Peter Scoulding

A CIP catalogue record for this book is available
from the British Library.

ISBN 978 1 4451 4749 9 (hbk)
ISBN 978 1 4451 4751 2 (pbk)
ISBN 978 1 4451 4750 5 (library ebook)

Printed in China

FSC
www.fsc.org
MIX
Paper from
responsible sources
FSC® C104740

Franklin Watts
An imprint of
Hachette Children's Group
Part of The Watts Publishing Group
Carmelite House
50 Victoria Embankment
London EC4Y 0DZ

An Hachette UK company.
www.hachette.co.uk